THE ROAD
TO SUCCESS
is Always Under Construction

Written and compiled by Larry Wall and Kathleen Russell

Published by
Walrus Productions

Published by Walrus Productions
4805 NE 106th St., Seattle, Washington, 98125.

Typography by The Durland Group

Printed by Vaughan Printing, Nashville

Library of Congress Catalog Card Number 92-93426

The Road To Success is Always Under Construction / written and compiled
by Larry Wall and Kathleen Russell

ISBN 0-9635176-0-0

Fourth Printing
Printed in the United States of America

INTRODUCTION

We have created this collection of favorite quotations and aphorisms in the hopes that others will share the inspiration, humor and reflection they have given us. As you travel the way to your own success, we hope the road always rises up to greet you and the wind is forever at your back. But if your road should get washed out or the wind defy your progress, then open this book. You will not find specific answers within its pages because those most often lie within ourselves. You will find simple reminders that we must all look inside for what we seek. Also, remember that breakdowns are a part of life - look for the value in them. Without breakdowns, there can be no breakthroughs.

"Happy Trails"

Kathleen Russell and Larry Wall

ACKNOWLEDGMENTS

We'd like to thank our parents, Ellen & Ronald Russell and Dorothy & Clifford Wall. We so appreciate the love, guidance, support, time, experience and encouragement you've given us throughout our lives. Thank you and we love you! To Steve & Margie Norman for their desk top publishing services, advice and your treasured friendship. To AMERICAN ARTS & GRAPHICS for publishing and distributing our poster of the same title. To many friends who have been encouraging and inspirational in our lives, Jo & Mike Turner, Rev. Bob & Joyce Mays, Kyle Winn, John Garner, The two Bobs (Wall & Solum), Camille Fulmer, Dixon Deleña, Sue Mays, Nicola Myers, Bob Staniford, Bruce Ungari, Guy & Cindy Nemer-Kaiser, Peter Vizzusi, Polly Dale, Paul Fleury, Ed Myers, Ona Rae Belzner, Trudie Dvorak, Frank Gallo, Don & Yvonne Ackley, Teri & Don Gillet, Rob & Chelle Stringer, Mike Henry, Neil Griot, Tim Jones, Bruce McDonald, Cubby, Steve & Lorraine Dobson, Linda & Gerry Powell, Gary Watrous, Denis & Judy Correia, Dave Norman, Peter Hebbron, Gil Schroeder, Luann Hamilton, Doug Hogue, Ken & Liz Bloom,

Bill Haworth, Dennis Koepke, Karen Hayes, David Kelly, Kathleen Odell, John & Carol Zarek, Casey Fuller, Joe Tall, Dan Kimble, Jerry Kemp, Dave & Nole Ann Horsey, Tom Staniford, Joe Hinchy, Nanook Papp, Judith & Thorn Ford, Herb & Lori Benty, Gail Gastfield, Ralph & Deanna Potts, Pam Bridgen, Mark Gilman, Dan & Rich Burgher, Tim Flint, Carl Rennie, Mike & Joyce Peterson, Ada Michelson, Rolleen & Fred Gockel, Pete Peterson, Harold & Elaine Miggitsch, Harold & Bernice Lamberton, Roy & Bevie Wall, Ken & Gina Hardy, Rick Smilo, Erik Wiitila, Bob Eskola, Wes Logino, Mark Leader, Rodolfo Arias and nos amigos a Jalisco's, CIE Photo, Willow, Vassily, Valéry, Oleg, Yuri, Burlaka, Roman, Susan & Paul Legacy, Naomi Bunis, Betty Smith, Jay & Linda Kordich, Barb Jefferson, Kay Held, Ed Gregory, Cathy Nelsen, Angie Oliver, Toni Snyder, Roy Record, Cindy Marcell, Jim & Mary Lou Terhaar, Ken Carlston and Ben Cording. A special acknowledgment to our brothers and sisters: Dennis & Janine Russell, Keith & Sandra Russell, Beverly & Martin Hopper, Cathy & Tim Burr.

We dedicate this book to our parents
with love

To Ronald & Ellen Russell
and
Clifford & Dorothy Wall

Few people travel
the road to success
without a puncture or two.

Diplomacy is the art
of letting someone else
get your way.

Life is not so much
a matter of position
as of disposition.

The happiness of your life depends on the quality of your thoughts.

A pint of example is worth a gallon of advice.

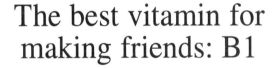

The best vitamin for
making friends: B1

Nobody raises
his own reputation
by lowering others.

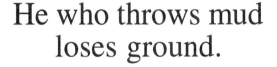

He who throws mud
loses ground.

A smile
is an inexpensive way
to improve your looks.

Most people
are about as happy
as they make up
their minds to be.

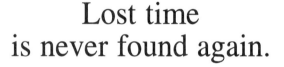

Lost time
is never found again.

One thing
you can't recycle
is wasted time.

Some people
develop eye strain
looking for trouble.

A hard thing
about business
is minding your own.

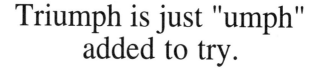

Triumph is just "umph" added to try.

Success comes to those
who make it happen
not those who let it happen.

Frogs have it easy.
They can eat
what bugs them.

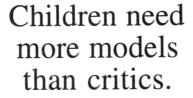

Children need
more models
than critics.

The pursuit of happiness is the chase of a lifetime.

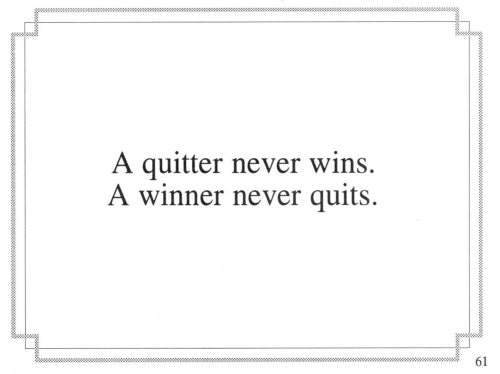

A quitter never wins.
A winner never quits.

If the going gets easy, you may be going downhill.

Don't let yesterday use up today.

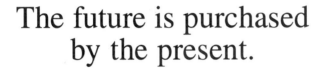

The future is purchased
by the present.

Ideas won't work
unless you do.

If you don't want to work,
you have to earn
enough money
so you won't have to.

Dieters: People that are *thick* and tired of it.

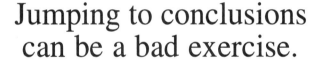

Jumping to conclusions
can be a bad exercise.

A ship in harbor is safe
but that is not what
ships are built for.

A turtle makes progress when it sticks its neck out.

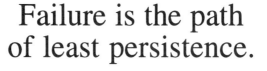

Failure is the path
of least persistence.

Hard work is the yeast that raises the dough.

Patience
is counting down
without blasting off.

Behavior is the mirror
in which everyone
shows their image.

Some folks won't look up until they are flat on their backs.

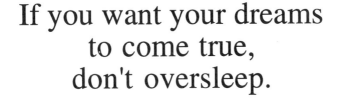

If you want your dreams
to come true,
don't oversleep.

Friend:
One who knows
all about you and
likes you just the same.

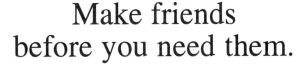

Make friends
before you need them.

Money talks
and often just says,
"Good-bye."

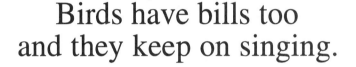

Birds have bills too
and they keep on singing.

Forbidden fruit
is responsible
for many a bad jam.

God's retirement plan is out of this world.

A good example
is the best sermon.

The Ten Commandments
are not multiple choice.

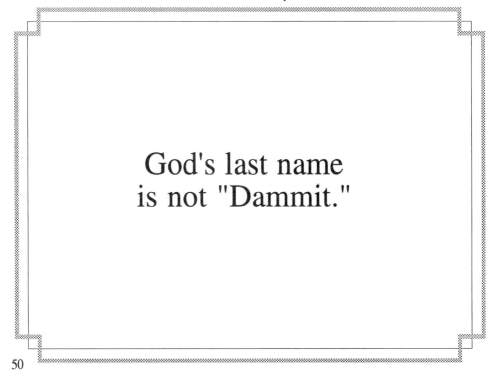

God's last name
is not "Dammit."

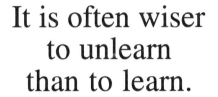

It is often wiser
to unlearn
than to learn.

Minds are like parachutes;
they function
only when open.

No man knows less than the man who knows it all.

It's nice to be important,
but it's more important
to be nice.

Live as you wish
your kids would.

Swallowing your pride
seldom leads to indigestion.

If you can laugh at it, then you can live with it.

People don't fail; they give up.

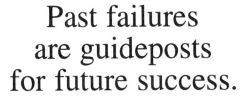

Past failures
are guideposts
for future success.

One who lacks courage
to start
has already finished.

If others have sinned,
you need not mention it.

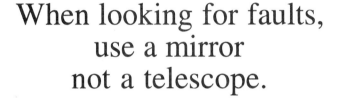

When looking for faults,
use a mirror
not a telescope.

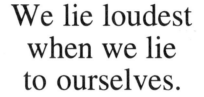

We lie loudest
when we lie
to ourselves.

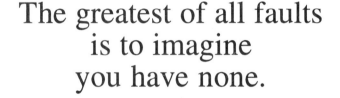

The greatest of all faults
is to imagine
you have none.

There is no right way to do a wrong thing.

It is much easier
to be critical than
to be correct.

He who forgives
ends the quarrel.

Having a sharp tongue can cut your own throat.

Smile,
it takes only 13 muscles;
a frown takes 64.

Of all the things you wear,
your expression
is the most important.

Kindness:
a language the deaf can hear
and the blind can see.

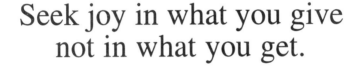

Seek joy in what you give
not in what you get.

Heaviest thing to carry:
a grudge.

It's not the load
that breaks you down,
it's the way you carry it.

Too many of us
speak twice
before we think.

If you must cry
over spilled milk,
then please try
to condense it.

Everyone has
20/20 hindsight.

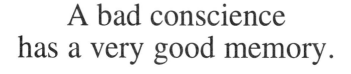

A bad conscience
has a very good memory.

The smallest good deed
is better than
the grandest intention.

The best way
to cheer yourself up
is to cheer
somebody else up.

Fear is the lack of faith.

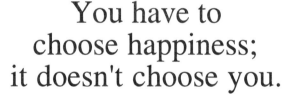

You have to
choose happiness;
it doesn't choose you.

Failing to prepare,
we prepare to fail.

Don't learn safety rules
simply by accident.

A smooth sea
never made a
skillful sailor.

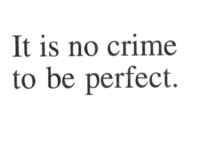

It is no crime
to be perfect.

Break a bad habit -
Drop it.

Nothing so needs reforming as other people's habits.

Feed your faith
and
doubt will starve to death.

If you're going
in the wrong direction,
remember,
God allows U turns.

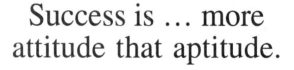

Success is … more
attitude that aptitude.

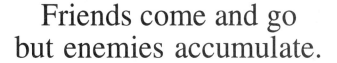

Friends come and go
but enemies accumulate.

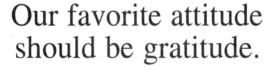

Our favorite attitude
should be gratitude.

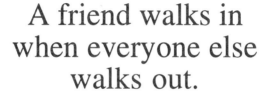

A friend walks in
when everyone else
walks out.

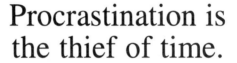

Procrastination is the thief of time.

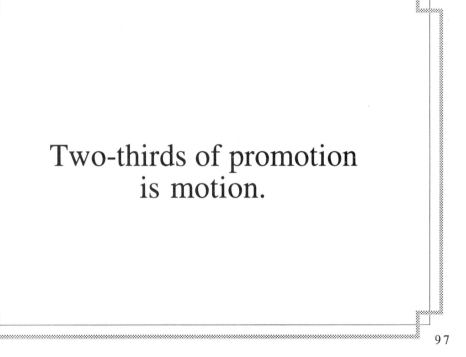

Two-thirds of promotion is motion.

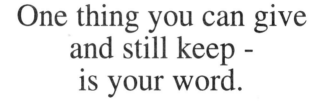

One thing you can give
and still keep -
is your word.

Action
speaks louder than words
but not nearly as often.

Success comes in cans.
Failure comes in can'ts.

"Well done!" is better
than "Well said!"

THE ROAD TO SUCCESS is Always Under Construction

The reward
for work well done
is the opportunity
to do more.

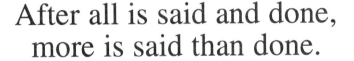

After all is said and done,
more is said than done.

You are rich according to
what you are,
not according to
what you have.

Your interest should be
in your future …
you're going to spend
the rest of your life there.

Just do what you
love and believe in
and it will come naturally.

Even if you're
on the right track,
you'll get run over
if you just sit there.

Even a stopped clock is right twice a day.

Be like a postage stamp;
stick to one thing
till you get there.

An angry man
opens his mouth
and shuts his eyes.

Anger
is one letter short
of danger

If you aren't
fired up with enthusiasm,
you will be fired
with enthusiasm.

The best time
to start thinking about
your retirement is …
before the boss does.

Tact is
the ability to see others
as *they* wish to be seen.

You are only
what you are when
no one is looking.

Tact is
rubbing out another's mistake
instead of rubbing it in.

Men give away
nothing so freely
as their advice.

Positive anything
is better than
negative nothing.

Who dares for nothing
need hope for nothing.

Kindness consists
in loving people
more than they deserve.

Hug your kids at home.
Belt them in the car.

All children are
born with a hearing problem.
They can hear everyone
but their mother.

If you want
a place in the sun,
prepare to put up
with a few blisters.

If you worry,
will it change the future?

Worry is
interest paid on trouble
before it is due.

The reason why worry kills
so many more people
than work … is that many
more people worry than work.

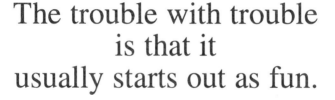

The trouble with trouble
is that it
usually starts out as fun.

It isn't
what you know that counts,
it's what
you think of in time.

If you don't care
where you're going,
any road will get you there.

Hire people
smarter than you.
This shows you're
smarter than they are.

Put your goals in writing.
If you can't put it
on a sheet of paper,
you probably can't do it.

You don't have to brush
all of your teeth,
only the ones
you want to keep.

Better a tooth out
than always aching.

The best way to determine what motivates people? Ask them!

When you
don't have an education,
you've got to
use your brains.

Experience is
the name men give to
their screw-ups and sorrows.

People that wake up and
find they are a success
haven't been asleep.

If you can't
tie good knots,
tie plenty of them.

Not doing more than average
is what
keeps the average down.

"I tried, but it didn't work"
is a lot better than
"I wish I'd tried."

There can be no rainbow
without
a cloud and a storm.

Where you come from
isn't as important as
where you are going.

Don't drive
as if you owned the road;
drive as if you owned the car.

Ride the horse
in the direction it's going.

You have
to forget about fishing …
if you want to catch fish.

THE ROAD TO SUCCESS is Always Under Construction

The worst itches
are always where
you do not want
to be seen scratching.

146

Sometimes, the money
you save "doing it yourself"
will come in handy for
getting it done over.

A bargain is
anything a customer thinks
the store is losing money on.

It is especially hard
to work for money
you've already spent
for something you didn't need.

Some people
have enough money
for the rest of their life
(unless they buy something).

Sometimes one pays most
for the things
one gets for nothing.

Usually when you're young,
you know everything …
except how to make a living.

Some people think a home
is only good
to borrow money on.

Money isn't everything,
but it sure keeps you
in touch with your kids.

Let us so live that even
the undertaker will be sorry.

Be nice to people
on your way up …
because you may meet them
on your way down.

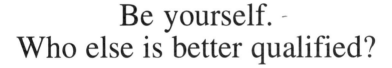

Be yourself.
Who else is better qualified?

May the road
rise up to greet you and
the wind be at your back.

NOTES

THE ROAD TO SUCCESS

POSTER AND BOOK ORDER FORM

THE ROAD TO SUCCESS IS ALWAYS UNDER CONSTRUCTION

22" x 34"

Please send me

_____ Books @ 7.95 = $ _____

_____ Posters @ 7.95 = $ _____

Total = $ _____

The book may be ordered through your local book outlet by referring to:
ISBN # 0-9635176-0-0

Price includes shipping & handling.
Check or money order only.

Send to: Walrus Productions
4805 NE 106th St.
Seattle, WA 98125

Name _____

Address _____

City/State _____ Zip _____

Price and availability subject to change.